THE
PREACHER'S
WORKSHOP
SERIES

Book 2

Letting the Word Come Alive

Choosing and Studying the Text

W. A. Poovey

Publishing House
St. Louis

Contents

Preface   3

1. So Many Texts   5

2. Taking Aim   12

3. That Alien Language   19

4. Not Our World   26

5. This Word and the Word   33

6. Special Areas for Study   40

Concordia Publishing House, St. Louis, Missouri
Copyright © 1977 Concordia Publishing House
Manufactured in the United States of America

Library of Congress Cataloging in Publication Data

Poovey, William Arthur, 1913-
       Letting the word come alive.

       (The Preacher's workshop series; book 2)
       1. Bible—Homiletical use. I. Title. II. Series.
BS534.5.P66   251'.01   77-21682
ISBN 0-570-07401-0

Preface

This book is one in a series of nine that deal with preaching. That word "preaching" immediately elicits some negative reactions from most people. "Don't preach to me" is part of our vocabulary. Yet the preacher is called on to preach (we hope without being "preachy") every Sunday, week after week. The written sermons for one year that come from his desk would easily fill a 300-page volume, and he, as well as his "regular readers," expect that each page will be as informative as tomorrow's newspaper and as interesting as this evening's TV special. This expectation of excellence is growing among a laity that is increasingly well informed. It is no wonder that many preachers feel inadequate about their preaching and panic when "the well runs dry." And it seems to run dry more quickly and more often as the years pass.

This is why this series is addressed primarily to the veteran preacher, although the beginning preacher will find much in each book that will help him also. Each author is an expert in his field and has been given the assignment of opening up his study door to the reader so that he can look over his shoulder and gain a new appreciation for preaching and sharpen the tools that he uses in his own "workshop." Appreciation for the pulpit as the place where God meets people through the vehicle of human language permeates each book in this series. Each author is committed to the power of the Gospel, a power that gives and sustains the new life that Jesus Christ purchased and the Holy Spirit offers. It is the goal of The Preacher's Workshop Series to get at the basics of that kind of preaching.

This series is designed so the reader can accomplish this goal if he simply reads and applies the offered insights. These books are also intended to encourage the preacher to enter into dialogs and workshops with his peers so that this series will provide the basis for continued growth in saying the Good News to the world that needs it so much.

So we open the door to you, preacher of Good Tidings. Welcome to the workshop!

The Preacher's Workshop Series

Book 1 — The Mighty Word: Power and Purpose of Preaching
Book 2 — Letting the Word Come Alive: Choosing and Studying the Text
Book 3 — The Real Word for the Real World: Applying the Word to the Needs of People
Book 4 — The Lively Skeleton: Thematic Approaches and Outlines
Book 5 — The Creative Task: Writing the Sermon
Book 6 — The Sermon as Part of the Liturgy
Book 7 — Power from the Pulpit: Delivering the Good News
Book 8 — A Sermon Is More than Words
Book 9 — Better Preaching: Evaluating the Sermon

Richard Kapfer, Series Editor

1

So Many Texts

The preacher stands in the pulpit and presents a twenty-minute talk about the situation in Israel today. Or about the strengths and weaknesses of the new morality. Or the blessings of the capitalistic system. Or the failure of modern parents to rear their children properly. At the close of his twenty-minute period he says "amen" and steps down from the pulpit and goes to the altar to continue the liturgical service. Has he preached a sermon on this Sunday morning?

Not really. For the Christian church has always been in agreement that the task of the preacher is to present the Word of God to the hearers. The preacher is a herald, a spokesman for God. As James Stewart puts it in his latest book of sermons, *King Forever* ([Nashville: Abingdon Press, 1975], p. 154): "I am sure the preacher's task today is not to propound theories and opinions. . . . It is to take this book (the Bible) and let it speak for itself." The preacher may or may not be an expert on world situations, on parental guidance, on matters of morals or politics, but his responsibility is directed toward God's message to His people, particularly as that centers in the person and work of Jesus Christ. As Luther said: "We preach always Him, the true God and Man. This may seem a limited and monotonous subject, likely to be soon exhausted, but we are never at the end of it."

Of course this does not say that the preacher has nothing to say about contemporary problems or about the world which exists outside the church. Christianity changes the whole outlook and viewpoint of a human being. It gives him a new view of all existence. In John Masefield's *The Everlasting Mercy* Saul Kane found that even the brook running past the railway station looked different when he had been converted. In a similar way the preacher may talk about the situation in Israel or any of the other topics listed above, but he does so only by seeking to bring the Word of God to bear on the subject. He must never desert his task, that of speaking God's Word to God's people.

In order to help the preacher do this, the church has developed the custom of basing the sermon on a specific portion of Scripture. There is no Biblical injunction to do this. Some of the sermons recorded in the New Testament seem to have texts, others not. And there have been times when textual preaching was not the practice of many preachers. There still may be a reason on a particular Sunday to preach a sermon without using a text. But the wisdom of the ages is in the custom. The use of a text greatly simplifies sermon making, and in these busy days if textual preaching did nothing but save the pastor some time, it would be worthwhile to follow the custom. Clovis Chappel, popular Methodist preacher, once said that just as the Israelites found making bricks with straw difficult enough, much less making them without straw, so sermons are hard enough to construct when you use a text and infinitely more difficult if there is no specific Biblical material to guide the preacher in his task.

It goes without saying that the reading of a text is no guarantee of a textual or even a Christian sermon. The realm of sermonic literature is full of homiletical horrors, of texts twisted and pulled to fit all kinds of ideas. Frederick Louis Allen, in a satirical article on how to preach a sermon once declared that any competent minister could arrive at any conclusion from any text. One almost feels that he is right in his harsh verdict. At least we can say that the integrity of the sermon does not lie in the question "Does the man use a text?"—but rather in the simple word "how." *How* does the preacher use his text? This is a matter for each man to consider carefully as he studies God's Word.

But suppose you honestly wish to proclaim God's truth to a congregation. Suppose you have decided that you will endeavor to deal honestly and fairly with a text, seeking to show 20th-century listeners what this portion of God's Word has to say to them. What then? How does one start?

Any minister, faced with the task of choosing a text immediately becomes aware that he is suffering from a profusion of riches. The Bible is a big book. No, it is a library, a library of religious literature extending over several thousand years of human history. Within this library are all types of literature, stories, poetry, proverbs, parables, etc. There are texts everywhere, enough to keep a man preaching several lifetimes without any necessity of repeating himself. But next Sunday there must be one text for one sermon and the Sunday after that a different portion of Scripture must be found for another sermon, etc. How do we make the choice?

In some ways, the simplest scheme for preaching is the "free text" method. The man who proceeds on this program studies the Bible faithfully, and out of his reading he selects those portions of Scripture which speak most directly to him or which seem to have a special message for his particular congregation. Each week then he chooses a special passage for his sermon text. He may during his study jot down a number of texts which he hopes to use sometime in the future, but each Sunday's sermon is based on a specific text picked for that week.

There are advantages to this method of text selection. The minister uses only those portions of Scripture which have spoken to him, and he thus has an eagerness to share the message of the text with his people. Everyone who has read the Bible knows how certain passages seem to leap out at you and almost demand to be preached on. They set our homiletical wheels whirring from the word "go." There are other texts which do not arouse much enthusiasm. Every preacher who has used a lectionary has asked himself: "Why did those fellows pick this text for this Sunday?" The free-text preacher has no such problem. He makes his own selection.

Moreover we all possess different temperaments. The passage which stirs you may say nothing to me, at least for the moment. William Cowper's hymn

> Sometimes a light surprises
> The Christian while he sings;
> It is the Lord who rises
> With healing in his wings;

can also be applied to the preacher as he studies God's Word. Suddenly the light may dawn for him, the truth of a particular passage may become clear, and he is ready to preach about this truth, where a few minutes before, the words were dull and almost empty of meaning. The free-text preacher is always ready to take advantage of these moments of enlightenment.

In addition, every congregation is different, and only the preacher knows what his particular congregation needs to hear at a specific point in time. But if he simply takes the text assigned for that Sunday, he may end up as the proverbial preacher did who answered questions that his people never asked and explained problems that had never bothered anyone. If the great need of a particular congregation is to hear comforting words about the forgiveness of sins, it is foolish to talk to them about living the triumphant Christian life. Free-text choice allows the minister to tailor his message and his selection of a text to the peculiar needs of his people.

Having said that, one must admit that there are also many difficulties with such a program. Free-text preaching demands a knowledge of the Bible that many modern ministers don't possess. The Word of God contains thousands of beautiful passages, and each one has a message for today. But the preacher who is not as familiar with the Scriptures as he should be is tempted to settle down to the popular sections such as Psalm 23, John 3:16, Romans 8:31 ff., the parables of Jesus, etc. There is nothing wrong with using such passages for sermons, of course, but the resulting diet may be monotonous for preacher and congregation alike.

Moreover, free-text preaching can be time consuming for the busy minister. Choosing your own text can use up hours which might better be spent in studying the text itself. Unless a person disciplines himself in this matter, he may face Saturday with no text selected or with several having been worked on and abandoned during the week. This kind of preaching preparation may resemble the man who started out to choose a Christmas tree in the forest, but each time he was at the point of selecting a tree, he decided to walk on a little farther since there might be a better one just ahead. He emerged on the other side of the forest, with no tree. The busy work schedule for the modern minister doesn't permit him to dilly-dally in the choice of a text.

But perhaps the greatest problem in selecting your own text is that we all have our religious hobbies. In the years when I taught preaching in the seminary it was obvious that even beginning students had their biases. Some turned out Law sermons almost exclusively, others were always Gospel oriented. Some were concerned about social issues, others stressed personal piety. Such leanings are inevitable. As one of the characters in W. S. Gilbert's *Iolanthe* says,

> . . . every boy and every gal
> That's born into the world alive
> Is either a little Liberal
> Or else a little Conservative!

Because of this natural leaning, it is important that preachers make sure they present a full and complete picture of God's truth to their congregations. But if the choice of a text as well as the sermon material is left to individuals, there is an increased chance that each minister will ride his own hobby horse. A pericope system affords no guarantee of a well-balanced preaching ministry, but there is more chance of variety there than when the choice of text depends on the preacher's whim.

Of course some preaching must be based on the free-text method. There are no formal lectionaries prescribing texts for funerals or weddings. Special occasions such as anniversaries and ordinations require the preacher to make his own selection of that portion of God's Word which is particularly fitting for a specific situation. There are of course books which list suggested texts for all occasions, but the final choice rests always with the individual minister.

And perhaps once in a while every preacher should have a fling in choosing his own texts. Perhaps he shouldn't do this for a whole year but at least for a season. Such a pattern of preaching will allow the man in the pulpit to speak on some passages that have special meaning to him. It will force him to ask, "What do my people need to hear from God's Word? What area of truth have I been neglecting?" Free-text choices may make the minister study his Bible more diligently, listening for the message which the Holy Spirit is seeking to convey to God's people today. Free-text preaching is not a good method for year-to-year ministry. As a variation, an experiment, a challenge, it has something to commend it.

One of the problems of preaching is that it is somewhat disjointed. Even the pastor who follows the church year pattern carefully finds that one Sunday he may be using a parable as a text and the next Sunday a miracle story may be the pericope selected. There is very little opportunity to do any consistent teaching through the Sunday morning sermon. Each message seems a separate presentation, almost totally independent of what was said before or what will follow.

One effort to avoid this disjointedness is the "series" method of making textual selections. There has been some effort to incorporate this type of preaching in the new three-year pericope cycle, but the simplest way to use the series system is to select a central theme or area of truth and then to pick texts that fit into the pattern. So the congregation may hear five sermons based on parables or six sermons on the fundamentals of Christianity or four sermons about the Christian home. This is a kind of free-text selection method, but there is some guidance as to the choice of selections. Almost all Lenten preaching is series preaching, but the technique can work equally well on Sunday morning.

Series selections can be closely related or very diverse. Thus sermons on death and resurrection may be closely integrated; sermons on Old Testament prophets might explore widely divergent areas of truth. Clarence MacCartney, famous Presbyterian preacher, used to preach on "Great Nights of the Bible," "Great Texts of the Bible," etc. Someone even constructed a series on "Famous 3:16s," based on texts that are found in the third chapter, the 16th verse of New Testament books. Such series have little coherence and only provide the preacher with some sort of hook to hang his ideas on.

But good series preaching has advantages. It offers the minister a chance to explore with his congregation an area of truth by concentrating the preaching on a special topic. There is some connection between sermons, and what is said one Sunday may help make the next week's discourse easier to grasp. If the series choice is a good one, people may make an extra effort to hear all the sermons on that subject. The preacher who uses a series may prepare a study guide to help his people understand what is being said, and thus study outside the morning service may follow. The new three-year pericope series with its concentration on a separate synoptic gospel each year has some of the virtues of the shorter series method, although it is hard to sustain a special interest for an entire year.

But as usual, there are difficulties. A series requires variety as well as continuity. The preacher must watch or he will repeat himself. Most series shouldn't include more than about six sermons consecutively, for we run out of good material by that time. Also, because not all of our members attend every Sunday, we may have to repeat material as the serial writer does, who prefaces each new installment with "the story thus far." In addition, anyone who prepares a series must be careful that the subject chosen will interest the entire congregation. A group of sermons on parental problems with teenagers may be helpful to some but leave the rest of the congregation completely bored. Too much of our preaching is aimed at married couples with children, thus totally ignoring the single, the widowed, the old, and the young in the congregation. It is difficult to do but the preacher is required to preach all of God's Word to all of God's children.

Yet using a series is a good method of choosing texts. It serves well in special seasons and also for presenting special areas of truth to God's people. The preacher here can integrate his study and his preaching so that as he learns the congregation learns. At times he may even ask for suggestions from his people as to areas of truth that they would like him to explore.

Now we must deal with the most common method of selecting texts—at least among Lutherans and those churches that use a formal liturgical service. This is the use of a lectionary or a pericope selection chosen by some specialists

9

in the field of worship. The new three-year lectionary which centers its textual selections in one of the synoptic gospels each year is an example, but of course it was preceded by many other types of pericope selections. In the useful book *Biblical Texts* by Paul W. Nesper fourteen separate lectionary series are listed, and several of these have multiple patterns for more than one year.

Most preachers are aware of the advantages of following a pericope system. It provides the preacher with his text each week so that he doesn't have to spend time looking for something to preach about. It enables the preacher to follow the church year in his preaching. It helps him cover the basic truths of Christianity in a systematic way. The use of the lectionary helps provide unity in the worship service. In addition, there are helps that have been prepared for most pericope systems, and every busy minister appreciates such helps. All of this is familiar enough and needs no elaboration.

But some other things need to be said. A lectionary program should not be regarded as a straitjacket. The individual preacher is always in charge, and that is as it should be. In some ways the pulpit is the last bastion of rugged individualism. There may be times when an individual lesson says nothing to the preacher. That's not the fault of the lesson. The preacher who tries and fails to find meaning in a text had better try a different one. After all, he owes his people a sermon on Sunday morning, and it should be a message that makes sense to the people assembled. Also there are times when a particular need may arise in a congregation. If the regular pericope does not fit the need, it is foolish to twist and pull at it to make it fit, and equally foolish to wait until a suitable pericope appears. Take another text.

It must also be noted that every lectionary system is caught between monotony and disjointedness. Most systems contain a series of Gospel lessons, another series of Epistle lessons, and perhaps a third round of Old Testament selections. But 52 sermons a year on one section of Scripture tends toward monotony. Mix the series and you get disjointedness. The nice balance intended by the originators of the pericope series is upset. And there is no way out of this dilemma.

The new three-year lectionary is particularly vulnerable at this point. It narrows the gospel selections to one author each year with fill-ins from the Gospel of John. The result is a concentrated study of the picture of Jesus as seen by Matthew, Mark, or Luke. This is useful for study by both pastor and people. At the same time the result is a somewhat concentrated and one-sided diet. So the preacher must decide whether he gains more in concentrated study or loses more through narrow selection. Each one must weigh the factors for himself.

Some have tried to escape this dilemma by using all three texts each Sunday. Of course the readings used in the service should be considered in sermon preparation. But if we are to supply the congregation with at least some exegesis during the morning sermon, it is difficult enough to do this for one text in 20 minutes. Three can prove a disaster. So we are simply driven to the conclusion that even the pericope system of textual selection isn't a perfect one. In an imperfect world we shouldn't expect anything else.

Having said all this, perhaps we can conclude this chapter by listing the marks of a good text. The following characteristics should be present. 1. A complete unit of thought, not a scrap of words. 2. Long enough to provide the preacher with some meat for his discourse, short enough to enable him to cover the material in one sermon. 3. As clear as possible. Some dark passages in Scripture may not be very helpful as texts. 4. Full of color. Life illumines life, and the more the text speaks of human life, the better it is as the basis for a sermon. 5. A presentation of the Gospel. Sometimes the Gospel message must be seen in contrast to or in fulfillment of the text, but there should be some relationship of the material to Jesus Christ. 6. A message for the preacher. As has been said before, if the text says nothing to the preacher, then he will say nothing to his people. 7. A message for God's people. Twentieth-century man is like first-century man, but he is also different. The text should speak in such a way that we can apply the message to our world.

And yet, the Word of God is a living word. Jesus said of the Old Testament writings, "They are they which testify of Me." If we approach the Scripture with prayer and thought, almost every text has something to say to us. The preacher has so many texts to draw from that he should never run out of ideas. The Word of God is a deep, deep mine with jewels rich and rare, as an old hymn says. The preacher who searches for the jewels will never be disappointed.

2

Taking Aim

Exegesis is a required course at almost every seminary in the United States. Almost all classes have as a part of their discipline learning how to dissect a section of the Bible, seeking to break it down to basic ideas, phrases, even individual words in an effort to extract the total meaning from Scripture. This is an important and necessary method of study for the preacher. But it is not the place where sermon preparation should start. Unfortunately the pastor almost instinctively begins, when he has decided on his text, to use the tools of exegesis. If he is skilled in Greek or Hebrew, he grabs for his Bible in the original language and begins his scrutiny. If his language studies have been neglected, he shakes his head, wishing that he had kept up with his seminary studies, and then he settles down to dissecting the English version. And all this is wrong.

For exegesis should not be the first step in working with a text. The preacher must take aim first. He needs to remember that his sermon is to be based on a unit, a section of Scripture. The Biblical writer used words, phrases, and sentences to convey a meaning to his readers. And it is this basic meaning which must first be ascertained. The Bible version which the preacher is going to use in reading the text to the people should be sufficient to grasp this meaning. After all, wiser men than the average pastor have translated the Biblical languages into an English version. If the translation is so bad that the general meaning cannot be grasped by reading the English, then the preacher had better buy a more accurate translation.

We do live in a fortunate time as far as translations are concerned. Biblical research into the original language has made possible a clearer understanding of the Word of God. The new versions often lack the grandeur of the King James, for example, but are excellent helps in ascertaining the basic meaning of a passage. The wise preacher purchases as many versions as he can afford and begins his study by reading his text in each one. If he finds general agreement, he knows he is in a position to try to get at the basic truth of the passage. If he finds some variations, he may note that fact and reserve his decision until he has done his exegetical studies. If he finds violent disagreement, then he may have to withhold judgment about the passage until he has done more work on it.

If a text is obscure, all the versions in the world may not help. I can remember that when the Revised Standard Version made its first appearance, I turned immediately to the Book of Revelation, hoping that now many hard passages would become clear. But when I finished my reading, I was not much wiser than when I first began. Translations won't solve all problems, but they can help.

A simple example will show what is meant. Recently a woman wrote to a church paper question box asking for guidance on Isaiah 45:7 (KJV): "I form the light and create darkness; I make peace and create evil. I the Lord do all these things." The passage sounded as if God were the source of evil and of sin, and this disturbed the letter writer. A quick comparison with other translations cleared up the mystery. Moffat said: "I bring bliss and calamity." The RSV rendered the key words: "I make weal and woe." The new American Bible Society version is "I bring both blessing and disaster." Not all problems can be solved so simply, but the preacher will find that the use of various English translations will often bring out the correct meaning and aid in an understanding of the basic truth in a text.

Thus the preacher needs to begin by looking at his text as a whole. He needs to grasp this essential unity before he begins like a small boy to take the watch apart. The preacher should read his text again and again, until he has almost memorized it. He should pray for understanding. Perhaps he should even sleep on the material before he begins his exegetical study.

Nor is this all. As the preacher looks at his text, he must ask himself these questions: Why is this story, this parable, this incident recorded in Scripture? What was the intent of the writer who penned these words? Why did the Holy Spirit preserve this passage for the church? We must always be aware that the Bible represents a very concentrated and selective view of human history. The Old Testament may seem a very large book to some, but obviously it touches on only a very selective group of incidents out of all the things that happened to Israel. The New Testament even makes a special point of its selective nature. John's gospel closes with the words: "But there are also many other things which Jesus did; were every one of them to be written, I suppose that the world itself could not contain the books that would be written" (John 21:25). Sometimes the synoptic writers simply summarize their material rather than giving us a detailed description of what occurred. Thus Mark 1:34 says, "And He healed many who were sick with various diseases, and cast out many demons." Why such a summary when on other occasions we are told the story of each individual who was helped?

Paul reminds us that the things which were written were written for our example. So it is a legitimate question to ask, "What is this passage seeking to tell the church? What is the Holy Spirit saying here?" Of course, we cannot always be sure, but the preacher needs to approach each text, believing that it contains vital truth which needs to be explained to God's people.

Often the clue lies in the context. The circumstances surrounding a story may tell us why this text is important or what it seeks to say. For example, the words of the godly Ananias to Saul, "Brother Saul," only become meaningful when you reflect on the fact that Saul probably had Ananias' name on his list of people who were to be seized and carried off to prison. When that is

13

understood, the single word "Brother" becomes a text in itself. What a witness to the nature of Christianity that it could make Ananias say such a word. And what a stunning shock it must have been to Saul to hear such a word from a man who had cause to hate him.

Not long ago I read the story of two preachers who were discussing their preaching methods. The first man insisted that he always examined the context first so that he would not misunderstand the thrust of a Bible passage. The other declared: "I never look at the context for fear it might spoil my sermon." That kind of preparation makes laymen declare that they can see no reason for their reading the Bible since they can't get out of it what the preacher finds there. The context must form a part of the taking aim even before exegesis is begun.

The preacher must also take another step as he looks at the text as a whole. He needs to consider the tone, the mood of the text. For mood is important. It can alter the meaning of a passage and can indicate the direction a sermon should or should not take. We are all aware of what mood can do in our daily life. A man can say something jokingly to a friend and then use the same words to insult an enemy. The mood makes the difference. Words repeated to someone else often give an erroneous impression because the tone of voice of the original speaker is missing.

Obviously as we read the Bible we have no way of ascertaining the tone or mood of a writer. Yet there are clear indications at times of what motivated the words of our text. It is easy to catch the note of exultation in Psalm 24 as contrasted with the despairing cry at the beginning of Psalm 22.

Or consider, for example, the story of Christ mourning over the city of Jerusalem. There is agony and love in the text. The words catch at the heartstrings, particularly when one remembers that Jesus will soon be put to death in the city that He loved so much. But because of this mood, it would be wrong to preach a sermon denouncing the sins of the Jews. The mood of sorrow must not be lost.

The story of Christ and the rich young ruler, as recorded in Mark 10, will be used as an example throughout the succeeding chapters because it exhibits many of the important truths that must be considered when studying a text. Any preacher who uses this story for his text must be concerned about mood. Note that the ruler comes to Jesus almost bubbling with eagerness. Yet he goes away sorrowing. Also Mark adds the significant words that Jesus looked at this young man and loved him. When those facts are considered, it becomes obvious that this story is a tragedy. The mood of the sermon must be that of sorrow, sorrow that so fine a young man could not take the one step that would bring him true happiness. It would violate the whole text to preach a sermon denouncing the evils of riches and the sin of greed. Mood here determines the direction of the sermon.

Or take a look at Paul's Epistle to the Galatians. This is a letter written by a man who is disturbed, upset by the backsliding of his converts. "I am astonished that you are so quickly deserting Him who called you in the grace of Christ and turning to a different gospel" (Gal. 1:6). "O foolish Galatians! Who has bewitched you before whose eyes Jesus Christ was publicly portrayed as crucified?" (Gal. 3:1). To preach a soft sermon about the comfort of the Gospel, based on a text from Galatians would be a total contradiction of the mood of the text.

One could cite many other examples. But the point should be clear—mood must be taken into consideration whenever it can be ascertained. Of course, when we apply the ancient words of the Bible to a contemporary situation, the circumstances may have changed so completely that a different emphasis may be needed. But at least the preacher should seek to decide what mood the words are intended to convey. Otherwise the whole spirit of a section of Scripture may be violated even as the minister seems to be paying lip service to the words. Some people can even make the words "I love you" sound like a threat rather than a declaration of affection.

But we are not finished with this matter of taking aim at a text. Although the problems of application will be considered in the next book of this series, there are some problems that must be faced even before exegetical study begins. The preacher must visualize the congregation sitting before him and listening to the text being read. What will be their initial reaction to the words of Scripture. Unfortunately in many cases the reaction would probably be a blank stare. It would be an interesting experiment some Sunday to stop at the close of the textual reading and ask the worshipers to relate what they heard. But some do listen and if they do, what are the questions which the text arouses for the listeners? Unless the preacher faces these questions honestly in his exegetical studies, the sermon will be a failure, no matter how well it is constructed or presented.

Let us take for an example the previously cited section from Mark, the encounter between Christ and the rich young ruler, Mark 10:17-22. At least three basic questions arise whenever anyone hears that text. The most vital is the relevance of this story to the congregation. The pericope ends with the words "for he had great possessions." At that point, about nine-tenths of the congregation automatically conclude that this sermon is not intended for them. They may settle back complacently, ready to enjoy the fun of hearing the rich members of the congregation get theirs this morning. And most of the rich members also are sure that they aren't meant either. They don't have as many great possessions as some others whom they know. This is the problem faced by the preacher, and unless he can find an answer to this question, his sermon is a waste of time. The departing worshipers may say, "Beautiful sermon this mroning," but the Word has not spoken to them. It has been a message for someone else.

The second problem occurs almost at the outset of the text in the little byplay between the ruler and Jesus over the words: "Good Teacher" (Mark 10:17b, 18). Jesus' reply, "Why do you call Me good? No one is good but God

15

alone," is a perplexing statement to our Lutheran people, who have been told again and again that Jesus is the divine Son of God. Is Jesus here rejecting all the views of the orthodox theologians of the church? It is not too difficult a question to solve. It may represent the clue to the meaning of the entire text. Jesus may be inviting the ruler to faith in the divine nature and to a confession that goes beyond "Good Teacher." It is worth noting that the ruler backs away and in verse 20 simply says "Teacher." He was not ready to go beyond that point and this may be the reason he could not accept Jesus' terms. But the point here is that the preacher as he reads the text must be aware of the problem and be ready to face it in his study and in his preaching.

A third difficulty lies in the terrible demand which Jesus makes of this ruler. "Go, sell what you have, and give to the poor . . . and come, follow Me" (v. 21). We may feel that the blessings of the Gospel are so much greater than the joy of possessions that the ruler shouldn't have hesitated. And yet every church member would quail before such a demand. Ask it of your members and see what the reply will be. They will probably say, "You first, preacher. Get rid of your television set, your new car and all your possessions. Then we will think about doing it too." I have often wondered what would happen if the rich young ruler asked for membership in a Lutheran congregation. I suspect that somehow we would find a way to get him to join. Yet Jesus' seemingly harsh demand stands in Scripture. The preacher who chooses this text must somehow deal with this demand, or his sermon is a failure.

The problems facing the preacher in dealing with this single text are formidable. Not all texts are so full of booby traps. Yet as the preacher takes aim at the text, he must be aware of any problems that must be dealt with, or he risks failure in his preaching. James Smart, formerly of Union Seminary in New York City, calls these questions the antitheme or antithemes in every text. They are the problems that our sin or our lack of understanding will raise against God's Word.

But how does the preacher decide where these rubs are in a text? For one thing, the preacher himself is a Christian and a sinner. He will do well to try to avoid a false piety, as if the idea that he would ever have any problems with a text is ridiculous. Despite our trust in the Word of God, we all feel at times that God is unreasonable or that certain statements in Scripture are hard to believe. We would do well to allow such things to surface in our minds and at times in our sermons. Even Peter was moved to confess that some of the things written by Paul were difficult to understand. Should we be less frank with ourselves. By posing as individuals who have no doubts, no problems with Scripture, we lose the common touch and in addition deceive ourselves.

But it is also true that the minister, because of his theological training may gloss over many problems that disturb the average church member. So here is where the laity can have their part in composing the minister's sermon. They can give their reactions to a text and often put their finger on a difficulty that otherwise would be missed by the pastor. Reuel Howe is an advocate of this

16

method of sermon composition and talks about it in his book *Partners in Preaching*. He advocates the formation of a group of lay people who sit with the pastor and study the text for a sermon before the pastor has begun his work on the passage. What they say may not be too helpful at times, but at least it gives the minister an idea of what the average person's reaction is to a text. Anyone using such a group should change the personnel from time to time, for if they become too adept and too theologically oriented, they lose their usefulness. Every group should be as catholic as possible, including in its membership young and old, educated and naive alike.

Perhaps we can finish this section on textual problems by noting two types of texts that occur rather frequently in Scripture. One of the most common is the persecution-type text. The New Testament is full of material of this kind. Jesus warned His disciples that they would have to endure tribulation and even death for the sake of the Kingdom. The Book of Acts is filled with examples of believers who suffered loss because they followed this new way. Paul in his epistles talks about his difficulties and also seeks to bolster the faith of his followers. Peter does the same, and the Book of Revelation is full of descriptions of terrible suffering that human beings were facing and would face for the sake of Christ.

It is obvious that such texts seem far removed from the life of the average Christian in America. Tell a complacent, self-satisfied congregation that they must suffer for their faith, and they will probably say, "Oh, we're ready. Bring it on." But they don't really believe it will happen, and neither does the preacher. The question posed by the old hymn:

> Must I be carried to the skies
> On flowery beds of ease
> While others fought to win the prize
> And sailed through bloody seas?

is usually answered by a "yes." What must the preacher do when faced with a text about persecution? No amount of careful exegesis will do here. How can such texts be made meaningful to congregations today?

There are three possible answers which the preacher can use. The first is to point out that God's Word doesn't say that every generation must suffer. There are times when the church is at peace. We can be thankful that we are delivered from persecution today and respond by showing our thankfulness through greater devotion to the Gospel. The second answer says that perhaps we need to examine our witness today. It may be that we are not being persecuted because we have softened our witness. The third answer says that Satan has found more subtle ways to plague the church and we must be alert to his strategems. But regardless of which answer the minister chooses, he must wrestle with this problem before he can make his text mean anything in the 20th century.

The second most common problem arises in the texts which deal with the Second Coming. Many of these texts are simple and clear as far as their basic meaning is concerned. Yet a problem occurs when we begin to preach such a message to a congregation today. It simply isn't true that most believers today look forward eagerly to the return of Christ. The last book of the Bible may end with the fervent prayer: "Amen. Come, Lord Jesus!" (Rev. 22:20), but that is not the prayer of people today. And the reason for the change in attitude is obvious. People in the first century lived short, unhappy lives. Many of the early Christians were slaves. The threat of persecution hung over their heads. No wonder they looked forward eagerly to the return of Jesus, for that meant a great change for the better. Today we live longer, are more comfortable, and are not therefore eager to depart from this world as we know it.

The key lies in the expression: "A change for the better." True Christians cannot be content with the world in which live. We are all tired of war, tired of thieving politicians, tired of sin and the consequences of sin. Thus the Second Coming promises us an end to the things that beset us, just as it held out promises of release to those first Christians. The preacher must contentrate his emphasis there and he will find that even these texts will have meaning to congregations today.

Thus we have seen in this chapter the importance of taking aim, of looking at the text as a whole, of considering its mood and its problems. The wise preacher starts early enough in his preparation so that he has time to let these things percolate in his mind. Of course all his work at this point is tentative. Careful exegesis may show that he has misunderstood the real thrust of the message. Solid research may show that the mood is different from what was thought at first. But if the original thinking has been done carefully, this change will not happen too often. And the sermon will gain a unity and a force which it would otherwise lack. Take aim before you fire!

3

That Alien Language

Everyone is familiar with the story of the old woman who declared: "If the King James Version was good enough for St. Paul, it's good enough for me." We smile at the woman's ignorance, and then there follows a feeling of regret. If only the old lady had spoken the truth. If St. Paul and the other Biblical writers had written in English, how much easier Biblical studies would be. If the events of the Bible had happened in America and if the characters in the stories and the men who wrote the various accounts had spoken English—what a beautiful dream.

But of course it didn't happen that way. The Bible was written in Hebrew and Greek, with a small section in Aramaic. Every word of this book is in an alien tongue. Moreover the languages of Scripture are not even remotely related to English except where we have borrowed from them. They don't even use the same letters as we do. The student of Biblical languages must begin by learning a different alphabet and in the case of Hebrew must even reverse his normal order of reading. When we consider all the grief that has come on mankind because of the events described in Genesis 11, we are warranted in concluding that what happened at the tower of Babel is one of history's greatest tragedies.

But there is no use crying over spilt milk. The Bible was written in a tongue that is alien to us. The sermon must be preached to our listeners in language that they will understand. A translation must occur somewhere between the original text and the Sunday morning sermon. So the question arises, how does the preacher proceed? Does he assume that translation is no business of his and that since he is preaching in English he must do all his work in English? There is some logic in that, but the church has always felt that the treasures contained in the original language are too great to be omitted in sermon preparation. The preacher who neglects Biblical language robs himself and his people of many valuable insights. Luther quotes Augustine as saying that the teacher who is to expound Scripture needs to know Greek and Hebrew, and the great Reformer himself declares that the one who doesn't have knowledge of the original languages may go about "like a blind man groping along a wall."

But we must be honest about this matter. Not all preachers have been trained in Biblical languages, and yet God has used some of them in His kingdom with great effectiveness. We pride ourselves on the fact that almost all Lutheran preachers have had some basic courses in Greek and most of them have also studied Hebrew. But we must admit that some were simply exposed to these languages without much happening. The old proverb about leading a horse to water fits here too.

Moreover even the student who was good in Greek and Hebrew in the seminary may not keep up his language study as he should. Most have good intentions when they leave school, but the pressure of the parish is very great today and one of the places where preachers often seek to shorten sermon preparation time is in the study of the alien tongues of the Bible. But this is dangerous, once it is started, for foreign languages have a way of fading into nothingness unless used. Language knowledge is like a muscle in the body—inclined to atrophy unless exercised regularly.

Perhaps we can help matters if we are clear in our own minds as to what we want to get from our Greek and Hebrew. At the outset, the preacher should understand that he is not trying to come up with a new translation, a new insight that no Bible student ever discovered before. Mere translation is of little benefit for sermon preparation. A careful reading of the English text will establish the basic thrust of the material.

A little incident will show what I mean. A number of years ago I took a refresher course in Greek at an eastern seminary. It was one of those cram courses in which you studied the language and nothing but the language day and night for five weeks. Each week you were sure you would collapse before the weekend, but by the next Tuesday you felt that the previous week had been a snap in comparison with what you were doing now. One day as some of us sat mulling over our translation of a New Testament passage, a music student walked through our study room, stopped, and said, "I have some information for you fellows," he declared.

"What is it?" we demanded to know.

"You fellows are too late. All that stuff has been translated before." Of course we chased him out of the room very unceremoniously. But he was right. It had all been translated before. And for rank amateurs like us it would have been foolish to attempt another translation if that had been our goal. So it is with the busy pastor. He gains no merit except a sense of accomplishment by simply translating the Greek or Hebrew into English. This will not aid him very much in sermon preparation.

But what *does* the preacher do with this alien language? First, he needs to make sure of the textual integrity of the pericope that he is studying. It is unfortunate that there are problems regarding the original text, but this is just one more evidence of the fallibility of human beings. Textual study is a very complicated task and is beyond the reach of the average pastor. He probably will simply have to accept the readings of the experts and proceed from there. But he does need to know what the text is that forms the basis of his study.

The next thing the preacher should do is ascertain where the problem areas are in translation. And here his study of the various English versions will help. For if all the translators agree on a certain way of rendering a passage, the student can be pretty sure that this is an accurate rendition. But when there is

20

conflict, then the fun begins. What is the correct wording? How should the translation read? Here is where the lexicons, the dictionaries, the grammars, etc., need to be consulted.

Let's look at our sample text, Mark 10:17-22, to see how this works. The very first verse of this pericope poses a problem for the preacher. The King James Version, the RSV, and the Jerusalem Bible describe the young ruler as asking: "What must I do to inherit eternal life?" Goodspeed translates the passage: "to make sure of eternal life." The New English Bible says, "What must I do to win eternal life?" Good News for Modern Man reads: "To receive eternal life." The Twentieth Century New Testament renders the passage: "What must I do to gain eternal life?" Phillips follows Goodspeed with the words: "To make sure of eternal life," while Taylor indicates how far his paraphrase is from a literal translation with the question: "What must I do to get to heaven?"

Of course, the basic idea is the same in each case, but there are subtle differences among the translations. "To inherit" fits well with our doctrine of grace, but there is no reason to believe the ruler was asking the question with a Lutheran emphasis. Goodspeed's "to make sure of" has a different note to it, as if the ruler had been through a spiritual struggle and never could seem to find any peace. The New English Bible with its activist "to win eternal life," contrasts strangely with the Good News version, "to receive." And the word "gain" as used in the Twentieth Century translation seems to fit very well with the character of a man who had great possessions.

What is the preacher to do? There are sermons in this simple variation in the translation. Of course, he immediately turns to the lexicons for help to check out the various wordings. He cannot simply add up the scores and choose the one that is favored by the majority since translators read one anothers' renderings and can be influenced for or against a particular way of stating a passage by their opinion of the previous translation. In this particular case we must admit that the lexicon isn't too much help since it indicates that the word used in the Greek means "to inherit, to acquire, obtain, come into possession of." So there is justification for all the translations. But the exercise has opened up all kinds of possibilities for the preacher.

This checking of the "hot spots" in translation can be helpful for sermon preparation. At times the bias of the translator will show by the choices he makes among various possibilities. At other times a whole new line of thought or approach to the text may come from a different way to read a particular passage. At least the preacher needs to check and see the possible variations in the rendering of a text. Even if this takes time, it also makes the Bible student think carefully about the fundamental meaning of the words he intends to use for his text.

Reading the pericope in the original language will also help show the flavor of the writing. Every language has its own flavor. No one would confuse German, with its long involved sentences and its ponderous verbs at the end of a passage with the light lyrical nature of Italian. Whether temperament influences language or language affects temperament, we can leave to the decision of wiser men. But you can learn something about a nation by listening to or reading its language. Unfortunately we cannot hear either Greek or Hebrew as it was spoken by people in Bible times. But we can gain some insight by reading a passage of Scripture.

The Greek Koine, for example, was the plain simple language of the people. The beautiful strophes of Hebrew poetry are almost entirely missing from the New Testament. The Gospel is stated in prose, and simple clear prose at that. One of the jokes of history was the effort by scholars to make the language of the New Testament fit the pattern of classical Greek. All kinds of rules had to be coined to explain unusual forms. What a relief when it was discovered that the language of the New Testament was not the classical Greek of Homer or Plato but the language of the people, the speech of commerce and of daily living.

The preacher who understands that fact will not be tempted to soar into flights of oratory. The metaphysical sermons of John Donne, beautiful as they are, simply don't fit the pattern of the New Testament. This does not say that sermon *ideas* must be simple. The Gospel of John will show that profound ideas and simple vocabulary can go together. But reading the Greek should discourage those purple patches which preachers often like to work into their sermons.

Also every language has its own peculiar grammar, and even grammar can help the preacher in his preparation. One of the problems translators face when translating from Greek into English is the different concept of time woven into each language. English divides time into past, present, and future. Greek thinks in terms of linear and punctiliar action. Every beginning student of Greek learns the difference between the aorist and the imperfect, but most translations don't pick up this distinction. Thus in Matthew 7:7 Jesus is really saying, "Keep on asking, and it will be given to you; keep on seeking, etc." What a difference in meaning the verb form makes here. And the Greek New Testament is filled with similar examples of places where the grammar affects what is being said. A. T. Robertson isn't exaggerating when he writes in *The Minister and His Greek New Testament* ([New York: George H. Doran, 1923], p. 20): "Sermons lie hidden in Greek roots, in prepositions, in tenses, in the article, in particles, in cases."

Even the little touches of humor are missing when we neglect the original language. The Bible writers play on words at times but this kind of thing can seldom be reproduced in English. Thus in the story of the rich young ruler Jesus makes the contrast between what the ruler has and what he shall have by the use of two forms of a Greek verb that differ by one having smooth breathing, the other rough breathing. Perhaps we should say Mark makes the difference in this way, since Jesus probably spoke Aramaic. One of the places where a touch of humor can be reproduced occurs in Acts 8:30 where most translations read: "Do you understand what you are reading?" Phillip really uses a play on words here, which C. H. Rieu picks up by rendering the passage: "Are you really taking in what you are reading out?" referring to the ancient practice of reading aloud. But most of these sly statements are lost for the preacher who deals only with English. And these little turns of language often help give the sermon a fresh note and keep it from being a dull prosaic restatement of things everyone has heard before.

But of course language consists of words. And it is in the words that much of the sermonic material is to be found. For there are implied meanings, undertones, and overtones in words. Gerhard von Rad puts the matter very clearly and thus exposes the agony of the translator: "Not a single word in the ancient language exactly coincides with the corresponding word in our language" (*Biblical Interpretation in Preaching* [Nashville: Abingdon, 1977], p. 14). The same truth is expressed in the prolog to the book called Ecclesiasticus, a part of the Apocrypha.

> You are urged therefore to read with good will and attention, and to be indulgent in cases where, despite our diligent labor in translating, we may seem to have rendered some phrases imperfectly. For what was originally expressed in Hebrew does not have exactly the same sense when translated into another language.

Thus, no matter how careful the translator has been, there are still hidden meanings that appear only after careful word study.

Word studies can do at least two things. First such studies will show where similar wording is found elsewhere in the Bible and thus aid the preacher in developing and illustrating his material. The fact that the same word is used in two different passages doesn't guarantee that they are related, of course, but it does open up possibilities for the preacher. A few examples will show what is meant. In Matthew 27:5 the word used for "hanged" when speaking about the actions of Judas, is the same word that is used in the Septuagint translation of 2 Samuel 17:23, where we are told that Ahithophel hanged himself. Thus there is a link between Ahithophel, who betrayed David, and Judas, who betrayed David's son, Jesus. Yet without a word study, it is doubtful whether the preacher would think of this connection.

Another example which also centers around Judas occurs in Matthew 26:49. Here we are told that Judas kissed Jesus. The word really means "affectionately kissed" him. But when we study the word we discover to our horror that this same word is used when the father of the prodigal welcomed home his long lost son. The word occurs in the account of the woman who kissed Jesus' feet at the home of Simon the Pharisee and also in the story of how Paul took leave of the elders at Miletus. What a shocking contrast in these various kisses, yet the same Greek word is employed in each case. A whole sermon can be based on this one word.

Word studies also yield valuable pictures for the preacher and pictures add to the richness of preaching. Note how often Jesus uses picture language—vine and branches, shepherd and sheep, the door, the way, etc. We sometimes say Jesus used that kind of language because He was speaking to Orientals. It would be more accurate to say that He used such language because He was talking to human beings and He knew that human beings think in pictures and in concrete terms, not in theories or logic.

Greek words often conceal interesting pictures. Thus the famous passage in Revelation 3:20: "Behold I stand at the door and knock," might easily convey the idea of a timid rap on the door of the heart. But the word used conveys the picture of knocking with a staff, in other words, Jesus gives a sturdy rap at our door. Again Paul writing to the Philippians in Phil. 4:1 calls them his "joy and crown." The word for crown has a double meaning. This is not a kingly crown but the crown given to a victorious athlete and the crown given to guests at a banquet on some special occasion. Either picture will convey special meaning for this passage.

One could go on and on. The preacher with a good lexicon has an almost unlimited supply of sermon material. William Barclay in his writings makes good use of this picture language of the Bible. All these glimpses make careful study of the original languages worthwhile for the Old Testament as well as the New also contains hidden riches for the preacher.

We admitted earlier that men differ in their abilities to handle the alien tongues of Scripture. But some riches are available even for the poor language student. The weak scholar may have to bolster his efforts with dictionaries, grammatical aids, even an interlinear. There are so many helps these days that even the student with no skill here can garner some of the riches of Greek and Hebrew. But the more we know, the more we can learn from Biblical studies.

We must still say a word about the use of this language study in the sermon itself. It should be obvious that all of this is preparation. It is not material to be lugged into the pulpit. Someone has said that a good sermon is like a good dinner. You don't need to know all the processes that have been carried out in the kitchen, or in the study, but you want to know that something happened there.

The preacher ought never use the Greek in the pulpit as a part of the sermon. This can have a bad effect on the congregation. They may feel that he is showing off his knowledge to them, slyly saying, "Look how wise I am," and that's not the goal of a sermon. Also references to the Greek or Hebrew may raise doubts in the minds of the members about the Bible that they read. They may feel that there is no use in trying to read the Bible since God hasn't given them the ability to read the alien tongue of Scripture.

How then can the preacher use this material wisely? The simplest way is to remind the congregation that all languages have their implications, their word sources, their deeper meanings. So it is only natural that this should be true of the Biblical languages too. There is a shading in the text this morning that translators could not be expected to reproduce, but this shading can help us understand what God's Spirit is saying to us through this word. By introducing material based on word studies in that way, the preacher can avoid offense and make the congregation see that what he is doing in this sermon is not pedantic or unduly scholarly but simply seeking to clarify the truth.

The alien language of Scripture creates a problem for the preacher. It makes his task more difficult. It forces the student of the Bible to dig into lexicons and dictionaries when he would much rather bypass such helps. But there are many compensations. The preacher should not overdo this kind of study and spend too much time working with the words of a text. But careful exploration of Greek and Hebrew will always be a rewarding experience.

4

Not Our World

The Bible is a very ancient book. It describes events that happened hundreds and thousands of years ago. No one can date the various books exactly, but most scholars agree that by 100 A.D. all the books of both Old and New Testaments had been written and were being used in some sections of the church. And 100 A.D. is a long time ago. A time traveler from that era would find our 20th-century world a strange and frightening place.

Despite the gap in time, the church has always insisted that the words of the Bible are living words. Men and women still find comfort and help in the Bible. The psalms still express the feelings and emotions of human beings. The ancient stories about Israel still have a contemporary ring. Above all, the message that comes to us from the cross can give us assurance of forgiveness for our sins and the Easter account can bring us the promise of resurrection.

Because the Bible can speak directly to us, the preacher may be tempted to ignore the setting of the text. He may try to rip the pericope out of its place and use the words as though they were written yesterday. But this is always a mistake. The Biblical world is not our world. The people who lived in that time had a different outlook on life. Their understanding of the universe was different. Their customs, their goals, their ways of worship were all different. And the preacher who does not understand that and who does not try to penetrate deeply into the world of the Bible may do an injustice to the text and the congregation. So let's see what we need to know in order to bridge the gap of the centuries between Bible times and today.

1. The size of the land. Because they hear so much in Sunday school and church about the land of Israel, most Christians have an exaggerated idea of the size of the so-called Holy Land. Actually, Israel never occupied much territory in the ancient world. The area that was settled by the twelve tribes when they came from Egypt was about 12,000 square miles, approximately the size of Massachusetts and Connecticut combined. And even a part of this, the coastal plain, was held by Israel's enemies, the Philistines. During the reign of David and Solomon Israel's holdings expanded to some 60,000 square miles, an area somewhat smaller than that of the six New England states. Immediately after the death of Solomon the empire shrank again and even split into two separate countries. So Israel was never large, never powerful or important in the ancient world. The people were seldom mentioned in the historical chronicles of that time.

Size alone is not important, of course. Yet Israel's smallness contrasts strangely with her boast that she alone worshiped the true God and that all the other religions of antiquity were false. It must have seemed absurd to the nations around her to hear the Hebrew people insist that they had the true knowledge of God. And that fact was even more peculiar when it was observed that Israel had no statues, no representations of her God. When the Romans finally invaded the holy of holies, they were shocked to find only an empty room there.

How different the picture becomes when we look at both Testaments from this viewpoint. Here we can understand what God meant when He said that He chose the Hebrews because they were the least of the people of their times. God's greatness and His patience with His ungrateful chosen people becomes more apparent when we remind ourselves of the size of the land held by Israel. Also our appreciation of those who remained faithful to their covenant is increased when we think of the prestige that the pagan gods must have had in the world compared to Israel's Yahweh.

2. The position of the land. There is a joke that is current about a modern Jewish politician who called Moses an idiot. When asked to justify such a statement, he explained that Moses picked as the promised land the only spot in the Middle East that didn't have any oil. The ancients weren't interested in oil, but they must have wondered at times why God chose the land of Palestine for them. For just as Belgium is often called the cockpit of Europe, Israel was and still is the cockpit of the Middle East. The Jews were always caught between powerful neighbors, Egypt on the west and Assyria, Babylon, or Persia on the east. There was no way to hide from their warlike neighbors. So they were always forced to choose between trusting in God or trusting in alliances with their pagan neighbors.

Despite this, they loved their homeland dearly. Jesus mourning over Jerusalem is a symbol of the Jewish love for that city. The singers in Babylon who could not sing in a strange land reflect this same spirit. People lived and died on the property that belonged to their family for generations. All this sounds very alien to our mobile society today, but the peculiar love of the Jew for his land and the peculiar situation of that land helps to explain many things in the Bible.

3. The land itself. The Mohammedans have a legend about an angel who flew over the newly made world with two bags full of stones. Over Palestine one of the bags broke and so that land got one half of the world's stones and the other half was distributed over the rest of the globe. The story says something about the land of the Bible. It says something about the shadow of a mighty rock. It speaks to us of a hot dry land where the sun beats down and even the shade from a rock is appreciated.

The Bible is full of descriptive material that grows out of the land of Israel. The image of the shepherd with his sheep is woven deeply into Scriptures. The strong emphasis on water, living water, is understandable only if you reflect on the nature of the land. The fact that the Philistines held the coastal plain explains the Jewish fear of the sea. It was foreign to them, and they therefore felt that only their God had power to calm the waves. Someone has called Palestine the fifth gospel, and although not every minister is fortunate enough to visit that land, the more he knows about the world of the Bible, the more alive his sermons should be. One needs to try to imagine what it was like to live in that world, to walk through dusty streets, unlit by modern street lamps, to travel the dangerous road from Jerusalem to Jericho, etc. The text comes alive for pastor and people when we understand the world in which the events happened and the words of Scripture were spoken.

4. The customs of Israel. Every nation develops its own customs, its own culture. Israel was no exception. And it is at this point that the Bible seems most strange to us. The whole argument about circumcision has an odd sound to our ears until we understand that God used this custom among Semitic peoples to serve as a mark of His favor. The marriage customs as described in the parables is not our way of solemnizing a wedding. Indeed the parables are often almost completely dark to us until we learn about Jewish practices.

To make it harder, Jewish customs changed over the centuries. The Book of Ruth contains sections that explain what the custom was when the events took place. Apparently already some of the old practices had changed by the time the book was written. The Bible is a very Jewish book, and Jewish ways are indicated in both Old and New Testaments. We may feel that there is truth in the couplet:

How odd of God
To choose the Jews.

But God did choose the Jews, and the books of the Bible reflect that fact. Adolph Hitler tried to remove everything Jewish from Christianity, but it was an impossible task. The preacher dare not make the same mistake by simply glossing over the customs that form the background of the Bible. The more we know about that ancient world, the better we are able to understand the message of Scripture.

5. The writing styles of the Bible. The Bible is not a book, of course. It is a library, a library that contains many different types of writing. Unfortunately preachers have not always understood the different styles and have misled their people because of their ignorance. Consider, for example, the poetic nature of the psalms and many of the prophetic writings. Our modern prosaic world doesn't have too much use for poetry and yet if we try to make prose statements out of many Old Testament passages, we end up with nonsense. Thus Isaiah 40:6 reads: "A voice says 'Cry!' And I said, 'What shall I cry?' All flesh is grass, and all its beauty is like the flower of the field." P. G. Wodehouse has one of his characters read this and then insist that its nonsense. He says that he has seen flesh and he's seen grass, and they aren't alike at all. Of course this is ridiculous, but so are efforts to take poetic sections of the Bible and force down on them a false literalness. The preacher needs to know what kind of material he is reading.

The gospels are also a case in point. Many Bible readers insist on making the gospels into biographies of Jesus. But they are not biographies. Nobody writes the life of a man and leaves out everything that happened to the individual between the age of 12 and 30. And nobody devotes almost half a biography to one week of a man's life. John sets the record straight when he says: "These are written that you may believe that Jesus is the Christ, the Son of God, and that believing you may have life in His name" (John 20:31). The gospels call for a response. They are not simply a narration of events. This doesn't in any way cast doubts on the accuracy of the things recorded but it does remind us what kind of literature we are dealing with.

The Bible contains historical material, poetic material, prophetic books, apocalyptic visions, letters, gospels, etc. The preacher as he studies his text needs to note very carefully what kind of literature he is dealing with and what the characteristics of that type of writing are. To make prose out of poetry or poetry out of clear factual statements is to do an injustice to the Bible and to the congregation who are listening for the truth.

6. The world view of the Bible. Bertold Brecht, the German playwright, has a memorable scene in his play *Galileo*. He shows the old cardinal meeting Galileo and condemning him bitterly for daring to suggest that the earth moves about the sun, rather than the other way around. And the cardinal's objection is that such a view degrades man who is the center of God's universe. The cardinal ends his tirade by saying, "I won't have it. I won't have it." But of course we have had to have it, whether we like it or not. Modern astronomy has opened up a different view of the universe than men held in Biblical times and in the time of Galileo.

Of course man's relationship to God doesn't depend on whether the earth is the center of the universe or not. Our relationship is shown by what God did for us on the cross. Nevertheless the Biblical world view is different from ours, and the preacher has to try to put himself in that pre-Copernican world when he studies a text. The universe has been revealed as much more complicated than Biblical man believed it to be. This has upset some people in their religious thinking. That shouldn't happen, for if people could grasp the glory of God in Old Testament times, how much greater should be our appreciation of our heavenly Father in His great act of creation.

Sometimes an effort is made to sneer at the world of the Bible with its idea of a three-story universe, etc. This is stupid. It is amazing to note how clearly the prophets understood God and learned about the magnificence of our universe even without our modern instruments for exploring space. But when the preacher studies his text, he should try to see the world as the people of the Bible saw it. And this should be done reverently, not with a superior air.

7. The problem of hindsight. We all know that hindsight is easy and yet unpleasant. The Monday morning quarterback can tell you how the game could have been won, even though the score was 40-0 against the home team. The bridge expert knows just where the wrong play was made, the investment

banker will be glad to tell you now what stocks you should have bought last year. But we don't always realize that we have the benefit of hindsight when we read the Bible. For we can look back and see the completed action and the results. The people whose stories are related in our texts always operated from a different basis and the preacher needs to understand this.

So from our viewpoint Abraham was very wise to leave his home in Ur and later in Haran, for as a result of those two moves he was blessed by God in many ways. But it probably seemed a very iffy situation at the time. So it is only by setting aside our hindsight that we appreciate what a witness Abraham is for real faith in God. Again Peter, Andrew, James, and John did the right thing by abandoning their fishing business and following Christ. But it must have seemed a much more risky business to them at the time.

Some of this hindsight causes us to judge harshly those who opposed Jesus. The typical Lenten sermon cuts to pieces the characters who were instrumental in his crucifixion. Yet Peter says concerning those who were involved: "And now, brethren, I know that you acted in ignorance, as did also your rulers" (Acts 3:17). We dare not be too confident that we would not have been among those who cried out: "Crucify him." Hindsight is so easy. But the preacher as he studies his text must try to put himself in the place of those who were passing through the events recorded. Only then can he grasp some understanding of the motives and goals of those involved.

8. The characters in the stories. The Bible is the most baffling and exasperating book ever written. It tells us all we need to know but not all we want to know about people. The material is brief, unadorned and maddening at times. For we are told so little about many characters and events. Thus the Book of Acts ends with Paul under sentence of death, but living and working in Rome, preaching and teaching about Jesus. What happened to the great apostle? Was he put to death or freed? Acts doesn't tell us. No modern editor would accept a book with such an ending, but there it stands to baffle us today. Acts also tells us about how the disciples chose Matthias to replace Judas among the Twelve. He won the choice over a man named Joseph, but that's the last time we hear about either of the men. They simply disappear from Scripture.

Erich Auerback, in his study of various types of literature called *Mimesis,* comments on the great difference between the Greek stories of Homer and the Old Testament stories about Abraham. He points out that when Ulysses returns home, his old nurse recognizes him by a scar on his body. Immediately Homer has to tell us the entire story of how the Greek hero got this scar. But in the story of Abraham offering up Isaac, we are told only the bare facts. We don't learn how Isaac felt, what Sarah said about it all; we are not even given any psychological insight into the mind of Abraham. We simply have the story related to us, and that is all.

Thus in a sense the Bible is distressingly brief even though it is a large volume. But this brevity can say two things to the preacher. First it can make

30

clear what the essential feature of a text is. Too many details might easily send the sermon off into all kinds of detours and side issues. That danger is reduced by the sheer simplicity of the Bible story.

Think for a moment about the story of the feeding of the five thousand. Can you imagine what a modern newspaper would do with such an account? There would be interviews, reactions, follow-up leads, descriptions of what happened to the left-over food, etc. But the event is described so simply by the gospel writers that you are hardly aware that a miracle has occurred. Jesus blesses the bread, has it distributed, the fragments are gathered up, and that's it. It's clear that it is Jesus who is important in the story. The food seems almost incidental. The preacher should not have trouble in identifying the real issue in most Bible stories since the material has been stripped down to the barest minimum of detail.

At the same time these brief stories allow the preacher to use his imagination in such a way as to make the characters come alive. How did Isaac feel about his narrow escape from death? What was Peter's reaction when he found he had been delivered from prison? The brief accounts at times almost cry out for some expansion. Of course, this must be handled carefully. Yet too often the people of the Bible seem like cardboard figures for us or even worse, like plaster saints. To make them come alive is difficult, but if the preacher tries to put himself into the place of the Bible character, he may help his hearers understand that the people in Scripture were human beings, facing the same temptations and enjoying the same blessings that we do today.

Dwight Moody was a master hand at this. Peter Marshall in his famous sermon about Elijah and the priests of Baal almost makes you feel like a spectator at that bloodthirsty scene. Such preaching holds the attention of a congregation and increases the chance of getting the message across. Of course, all such embroidery should be labeled as such. But we have one goal—to make vivid to a congregation the truths of the Scripture.

We have listed a number of ways that we can enter into the world of the Bible. Once again this is sermon preparation. Not too much of this material may appear in the final product. After all, explanation never saved any souls. But you cannot grasp the whole meaning of a text until you see it from the viewpoint of those to whom the words were first written. The preacher must live in two worlds, that of the Bible and that of the 20th century. But it is possible to get too immersed in the Biblical world. One writer tells about a preacher who told his congregation more about the Persian empire than he did about their daily problems. This is a matter of balance. But the wise preacher is seriously concerned about understanding the world in the Bible. For it is not our world, and the Bible itself can only be understood when we involve ourselves in its problems, its thought forms, its people.

Fortunately we live in a day when there are vast resources to help the Bible student. Archaeological research has shed light on many of the dark corners of the Bible. Visual material is available to acquaint the preacher with what the

Bible lands look like. Commentaries, study guides, etc., are being printed in ever increasing numbers. The minister who does not understand the Biblical world has simply cut himself off from the helps available.

A number of years ago there was a radio program entitled "You are there." It is this feeling that should guide the minister as he studies his text. He should enter into the events to such an extent that he truly feels that he was present when the words were spoken or the event occurred. Only in this way can he make the congregation understand the message of Scripture.

5

This Word and the Word

The previous chapters have dealt with what is usually labeled exegesis or Bible study. Now we need to see that systematic theology, dogmatics, doctrine, call it what you will, also must play a part in the study of a text. For no section of Scripture exists by itself. The word *pericope* tells us what a text really is—a section cut around or cut out of the Bible. But when we put the spotlight on one part of the Word, we do not forget about all the rest. Every text must be viewed as a part of the whole. Otherwise we can fall into the same error as the blind men who examined the elephant and ended with hopelessly distorted pictures of that beast.

Before we see how this word fits with the Word, we need to recognize that each text is unique. Each statement of Scripture has its own meaning, and that meaning must be explored and developed in preparing a sermon. Preachers get into difficulty when they ignore this uniqueness. Too many ministers simply note the general area of truth discussed in a passage and let it go at that. Thus if a text says something about faith, we get a general sermon on faith. But such an approach not only bypasses the special truth of an individual text, but it also ruins a number of other texts which also talk about faith but in a slightly different way.

Here is the explanation for men who feel that they are preached out, that they have said everything that can be said from the pulpit. This was the fatal weakness of topical preaching which seems to have lost its appeal in these days. There are just so many topics and when the preacher has touched on them all, he needs to move to another congregation and start over. But unless the student of Scripture looks for the unique message of a text, he may read and base his sermon on a portion of the Bible and still end up as a topical preacher. Simply seizing on a general idea in a text may save time for the moment, but this is a dangerous shortcut that will eventually take its toll.

Sometimes the preacher suppresses the unique message of Scripture for doctrinal reasons. We all know the kind of mind which says, "My mind's made up. Don't confuse me with the facts." This kind of thinking gets into the church too. There are hard passages of Scripture which seem to disturb our carefully laid out dogmas, and it is sometimes easier to ignore what is said than to seek to understand it. Thus Jesus' great picture of the Judgment as described in Matthew 25:31-46 may seem to challenge our faith in salvation by grace and the preacher may be tempted to gloss over the message of this text rather than come to grips with its true meaning. But this makes for dull and even dishonest preaching. The Word of God must be allowed to have its say. We ignore its message at our peril.

Let's take a look at some similar passages and see how much richer our preaching becomes when we look for the unique message in each text. The gospels record three instances of Jesus raising the dead: the story of Jairus' daughter (Mark 5:22 ff. and Luke 8:41 ff.); the raising of the widow's son (Luke 7:11 ff.); and the restoration of life to Lazarus (John 11:1 ff.). How easy it would be to choose a theme such as "Jesus, the Lord of Life and Death" and preach virtually identical sermons for each miracle. Such a sermon would probably sound very textual and would convey a proper message to the congregation.

Yet each of these three stories is unique and has features not found in the other two. The story of Jairus' daughter is interrupted by the healing of a woman who had an issue of blood. So here Jesus uses his power to assist an important figure in the community and to heal a woman who had been impoverished by her efforts to find help elsewhere. In both miracles the situation seemed hopeless, yet Jesus dealt with the human need. Also the words of Jesus to Jairus, "Do not fear, only believe," can make the text apply to every situation in life. And of course this story is an answer to all who mourn the death of a child and think that God arbitrarily took their loved one from them. For it is obvious that God does not want a world in which tragic things happen, and Jesus here gives us a glimpse into an eternity where death will be abolished forever. It is obvious that there are preaching truths in this text that make it unique.

Now look at the story about the healing of the widow's son. The pericope is very brief, but it contains the striking words: "He had compassion on her." Here we see the Son of God moved to action by someone's need. He did not know this widow, He apparently had no contact with her either before or after the miracle, but He was moved by her grief. William Barclay says that this story is in some ways the loveliest in all the gospels. Incidentally, here is a place where Greek can be of use to the student. Checking the original language will show that Jesus didn't say, as the RSV translates, "Do not weep." He said "Cease your weeping," or "Do not go on weeping." The tears were already flowing. And an understanding of life in the first century will help us to understand the widow's plight. This was her only son, and a woman with no husband and no children was a pitiful figure in that day. And Jesus had compassion on her. How different the sermon becomes when we look for the special features in each text. One could preach on these two miracles on successive Sundays and not repeat a single thought.

The familiar story of the raising of Lazarus also has its special areas of truth. What a marvelous story it is, filled with crosscurrents of human emotion. We note the message of Lazarus' illness brought to Jesus and our Lord's confident assurance. We note Jesus' calmness, staying to work two more days and then starting for Bethany. We see Jesus going to Lazarus' home

34

despite the threats against His life. We see with dismay that the disciples again fail to understand His intent. We read of Thomas' bold words: "Let us also go, that we may die with him" (Lazarus, John 11:16). All this takes place even before we are at the scene of the death.

Then we have the marvelous confrontation between Martha and Jesus. She is no longer the busy housewife; she is a woman who has lost a brother. But as she talks to Jesus, He draws from her one of the great confessions of faith recorded in the Bible. Then comes the meeting with Mary, the weeping by her and by Jesus, the prayer of Jesus, and at last the restoring to life. If one looks at the section that follows, it is apparent that miracles don't promote faith in all hearts, for the raising of Lazarus seals Jesus' death warrant. What possibilities are found in this one text! It is unique, and its unique features should not be brushed aside.

This then is an important factor for the preacher to consider. Every text has its own flavor, its own message. It should not be flattened out into a general statement of truth. The minister should ask himself what the Holy Spirit wants him to say, based on this particular pericope. Only when he does this can he use the text aright, and out of the uniqueness of the text comes preaching material for a lifetime.

And yet, and yet. A text does not float. It has no existence by itself. The Bible is not a collection of heterogenous elements thrown together. The Bible is a presentation of God's way of salvation for His lost and estranged children in this world. And a text must therefore be seen in relationship to the entire Word of God. It is possible to make the unique features in a text too unique by ignoring everything else said in Scripture. Thus one could seize on Jesus' words to the rich young ruler: "Why do you call Me good? No one is good but God alone," and make this passage into a denial of the divinity of Christ. But we don't dare do that, for there are other passages that say just the opposite. And we believe that the Scriptures present a consistent picture throughout.

This consistent picture is often called the analogy of faith. It means that the uniqueness of a text must not be stressed to a point where it denies the basic truths of the Bible. We must not preach salvation by grace one Sunday and salvation by works the next. We cannot make God a cruel judge in one sermon and then turn around and picture Him as a loving father a few weeks later. But how do we avoid this? How can we maintain the uniqueness of a text and still keep it in harmony with all of Scripture?

Perhaps the first thing that must be done is to make sure that we understand what is being said. If James seems to contradict Paul, then we should be sure that we understand both men. If a text seems to say something that doesn't fit with our theology, then we should check our exegesis and our theology. Many of the great quarrels in the church could have been prevented if all had made a more careful check of what they were really saying. The picture of judgment as described in Matthew 25 does not clash with the

35

doctrine of salvation by grace if we understand both the passage and the doctrine.

"Circumstances alter cases," we say, and that expression is a help in Bible study. A careful consideration of the context may show us how to make the whole pattern fit together. Thus Jesus says that He was sent only to the lost sheep of the house of Israel, yet these words contrast strangely with the universal message of the Gospel. But Israel was entitled to her chance to hear the Gospel first, for Israel was supposed to be the nation chosen to share the Good News with others. When we see the pattern of God in action, the two views are not inconsistent.

When the preacher studies the text, he also seeks other passages of the Bible to help explain what is being said. Thus when Jesus tells the rich young ruler to give all his goods away, we can ask whether this same demand is made for all who enter the Kingdom. A study of related passages will show that Peter still had a house even after he chose to follow Jesus. Zacchaeus made a generous offer to give one half his goods to the poor, but he did not give up everything when he became a follower of Christ. On the other hand, following this text Peter does say, "Lo, we have left everything and followed you," and Jesus did warn a man who wanted to follow: "Foxes have holes, and the birds of the air have nests; but the Son of Man has nowhere to lay His head" (Matt. 8:20). So we do not have to demand complete surrender of possessions by all church members, but there are some warnings in Scripture that such a surrender may become necessary. A good concordance will help make clear the meaning of a certain passage.

It is also important that we understand the gradual unfolding of Biblical truth. Progressive revelation has often been used to explain the Bible in such a way that it all seems the work of man who grows wiser down the centuries. This is nonsense. But there is growth in understanding in the Scriptures. The Old Testament often stresses physical rewards while the New Testament places the emphasis on spiritual matters and warns that we may even lose the physical things by the very fact that we are Christian. There is little stress on resurrection in the Old Testament. How could there be when the real guarantor of the resurrection hadn't even been born yet? This is why it is important to know the circumstances of the Biblical world, as emphasized in the previous chapter. Some passages must be explained by saying, "But we have later light on this subject." When this is considered, the uniqueness of a passage may be understood, and the message may fit very well in the analogy of faith.

We must also confess that there are times when the preacher is baffled. Peter found some of the writings of Paul difficult to understand. Luther insisted that he could find no explanation for the fourth word from the cross. "How could God desert God?" he asked. There are times when a Bible passage may seem too unique and we may find no way to make it fit into the realm of Christian truth. The preacher may have to say, "I don't know what to make of this." Perhaps when that happens it would be wiser to take another text, and yet it can be a helpful thing for a congregation to hear the preacher admit that there are some things in the Bible that he doesn't understand yet and some subjects on which he is praying for more light. I once had a seminary professor who told us: "I'm glad I have a God so big that I cannot understand him." None of us thought any less of the man for that candid admission.

So we must be aware of a certain tension in a text between the word before us and *the* Word itself. The preacher must not lose the specific message of the text nor allow it to be watered down into platitudes. At the same time each text is only a segment of truth, a small part of the whole, and the preacher must step back and see the whole picture. The old New England preachers who went for hours at a time in their preaching solved this problem by starting their sermons with creation and working their way down through the Bible until they came to their text for the week. Heaven help the people when the text was from Revelation! We do not have that task or that privilege. But the preacher must do this in his study. He must see the specific part and also the whole picture.

Now we must see another aspect of doctrine and its meaning for the preacher. Lutherans, following the example of the great Reformer, tend to think in terms of Law and Gospel. All of life seems to be divided into these two terms. Even children in catechetical instruction are taught to make this division as they study the Bible. There is nothing wrong with such theology, but the conjunction of the two terms has often misled the preacher. We get the notion that we can do one or the other—preach the Law or preach the Gospel. Such a view is a shocking misunderstanding of the relationship between these two terms.

The Law, as Paul reminds us, serves to bring us to the Gospel. Its purpose is to show man his sin and to make us feel our need for the saving grace of Jesus Christ. A sermon that is all Law is a worse than useless thing. If the congregation is left saying, "What must I do to be saved," and are not told, "Believe on the Lord Jesus Christ," then that is a wicked sermon. The text may only contain Law but it must be seen in the light of the entire Word, and that means that the Gospel must be included.

Dwight Moody in one of his writings tells how he learned this lesson very emphatically. One Sunday night he preached a sermon on sin and its consequences. At the close of the sermon he told his hearers: "Come back next week, and I'll tell you how to get rid of sin." That seemed a clever stunt to bring the people back again. But as Moody walked to the door of his meeting place, he noted that the sky was red. It was the beginning of the Chicago fire. Moody said, "I never saw that audience again. And I never made that mistake again."

Even though you may not have to worry about a fire wiping out your congregation, the fact remains that the Law by itself is of no value. It can drive to despair, but that is not the intention of the preacher. Even worse, the Law can make us feel self-righteous. Often a congregation enjoys getting a lambasting about their sins. They let the preacher take the hide off them, and

37

then they go out the door and say, "Beautiful sermon this morning, Reverend." The preacher has made them feel that they have suffered a little for their sins, and so they must be a little better than when they came to church.

But it is the Gospel that contains the words of life. The preacher is God's messenger to proclaim the Good News. And somewhere that news must be presented to a congregation. Some people feel that the constant proclaiming of forgiveness may come under Bonhoeffer's indictment of "cheap grace." That doesn't follow, and the answer to cheap grace is not "no grace." Every text must be examined in the light of the Gospel. A few years ago Lutheran ministers were shocked to read from a survey that a large number of their members thought they were saved by their own works. The preachers couldn't understand it. Yet they had to take some of the blame, for in an effort to be textual they had forgotten that the Law dare not form the entire content of a sermon. The Gospel must be presented, or the sermon is not Biblical or Christian.

One of the illustrations that I have always used with Junior homiletics classes in the seminary consisted of three simple drawings, each one to illustrate a way of understanding the Bible. The first drawing consisted of a series of unconnected lines. This illustrates the Bible view which uses each verse or pericope as a separate bit of truth. Obviously this is not the Christian view of the Scriptures. The second drawing was a long line, divided into sections such as creation, the fall, redemption, sanctification, etc. This is the dogmatic approach to Scripture, and too much Lutheran preaching follows this pattern. The third illustration was a circle with various lines radiating from the center. This view sees the Bible as a book with a center, Jesus Christ, and all Biblical truth finds its starting point there. This is the correct view for the preacher.

This was what Paul meant when he insisted that he would preach nothing but Christ and Him crucified. This is what Jesus meant when He said of the Old Testament that the writers there testified of Him. And this is the correct view which a preacher must have as he approaches any text. He must find the connection between the text and Christ. This does not in any way limit the preacher. He can talk about all kinds of truth. But Christianity finds the center of truth in Christ.

It is easy to see how this works. The opening chapters of Genesis speak of creation, but the preacher cannot speak of these without remembering the opening of the Gospel of John, where we are told that nothing was made without the Son being involved. The choice of Israel as a special people for God seems irrational and arbitrary until you remember that Israel finally became one person—Jesus Christ. Every moral injunction in the Bible takes on meaning because of our relationship to Christ. Thus we don't steal, not just because it's wrong and the commandment forbids it, but because stealing involves hurting our neighbor, for whom Christ died.

I once heard a student at Union Seminary in New York City preach a very

38

good moralistic sermon to a class. The late Paul Scherer, after complimenting the student on what he had said, pointed across the street and declared: "There's a Jewish seminary across the street. If you want to preach like that, they'll welcome you. But here we preach Christ." Hard medicine? No doubt. Yet Dr. Scherer was correct. The preacher as he approaches a text must ask first, last, and always, "What does this say about Christ? How does this fit with the message of Christ?"

This does not mean that the preacher tries to find all kinds of hidden references to Christ in the text. He does not have to resort to the age-old dodge of allegory. But the preacher sees the text in the light of Christian truth, and that means that Christ is found there. Sometimes Lutherans are accused of being second-person Unitarians. That's not a fair charge, but if the accusation implies that we should talk less about Jesus Christ, then we will have to accept the definition. For He is truly the way, the truth, and the life. The doctrine of Christ must be considered when we examine any text.

6

Special Areas for Study

The last chapter stressed that every text is unique and conveys its own message and poses its own problems. This is true, but there are also common problems raised by certain types of material in Scripture. No one would approach the Old Testament in exactly the same way as the New. Miracles require a different technique than parables. So in this final chapter on deriving material from the text, we will seek to explore a few special areas and see if we can devise some guidelines for certain types of pericopes.

The Gospel Parallels

Every Bible student is aware that the four gospels are not four different stories but that each writer uses many accounts that are similar to those found elsewhere in one of the other gospels. This is particularly true of the first three gospels, the synoptics, but even John contains some repetitions of the accounts.

If the stories were identically worded, the preacher would have no problem here. But that isn't true. The stories appear in different sequence and each writer includes details that are not recorded elsewhere. Thus in Matthew the story of the lost sheep serves to stress the importance of little children in God's Kingdom; in Luke this parable is used to refute those who were complaining that Jesus received sinners and ate with them. Again John places the cleansing of the temple at the beginning of Jesus' ministry; the synoptics include the story among the events of the last week of Jesus before His crucifixion. The Easter accounts drive exegetes wild when they try to draw up an organized narration of the events of that day. How does the preacher deal with these diversities?

Let us begin by saying that these problems don't belong in the pulpit. A sermon is not a lecture on the synoptic problem. The preacher seeks to bring the message of the text to people who are seeking to know God's will for them, and that message is not affected by problems of arrangement or the existence of differing details in a story. In the study the preacher may thrash out the issues for his sermon but he should not bring up such matters in the pulpit.

As a matter of fact, some of the problems raised by the four gospels have been argued for centuries. The final answer will not be known until Judgment Day, and then it won't make any difference. The Biblical writers have shown themselves to be wonderfully accurate, and we can put our trust in their words, even if we can't explain every detail in every story.

But let's look at the positive side of this matter. The existence of several accounts of the same event often helps us to fill out the complete story. Thus we can be thankful that we have three versions of the rich young ruler story since only Matthew tells us that he was young, only Luke relates that he was a ruler, and Mark alone gives us that beautiful sidelight that Jesus loved him. The preacher would be negligent if he looked at only one gospel writer and passed over the others.

On the other hand, no one is required to use all the parallel material. The text for a Sunday is from one gospel, not three or four. If the story is complete as it stands, the preacher may concentrate on that pericope. Thus Mark gives us a very short account of Jesus' temptation. It is not necessary to use the expanded versions in Matthew and Luke unless you want to. Matthew's use of the lost sheep story is perfectly valid, for the parable can be used to stress God's love for little children. The Lukan version can be ignored.

The only exception to this occurs when a parallel or earlier account may correct a misconception. For example, it would be misleading to use Matthew's story of the rich young ruler to blast that young man since Mark tells us that Jesus loved him. Or again, the synoptics tell us of the call of Peter, Andrew, James, and John, and the story seems to indicate that this was the first contact the men had with Jesus, although it does not say so in so many words. But the Johannine version shows that this was not the case. So it would be misleading to try to praise the four disciples for their instant surrender to the call of Christ. I have heard preachers try to do this, but it is poor preaching. We do not need to manipulate material in this way.

So the gospel parallels can be of real help for the minister in preparing his sermon. He should always consult them. A good harmony can be of great use and will save endless leafing back and forth. But this material is generally for sermon preparation and only by choice need the preacher bring in the other accounts for sermon illustration and clarification.

The Parables

Perhaps nothing is more characteristic of the teaching of Jesus than the parables. And perhaps nothing is more typical of the Christian church than the endless quarrels over the meanings of these simple stories told by Jesus. The church has swung from allegorizing every last detail of the story to trying to strip away anything that someone felt was added by the writers of the New Testament. And still the stories stand there, beautiful in their simplicity and yet profound in their depth of spiritual truth.

There are countless books about these stories told by Jesus, and so it isn't necessary to say too much here. However, a few points may be helpful. One thing that must be noted is that sometimes the sting of the story is gone today. When Jesus first spoke these stories, they must have struck home to His hearers with great spiritual power. Unfortunately we have heard them so many times that the impact isn't quite so great. We all know about the good Samaritan and the prodigal son. We have heard sermons about the sower and

41

about the man who found a treasure in a field. The preacher today is born too late and has a problem here. To increase his homiletical burden, the parables are filled with references to the customs of the first century and therefore require explanation which slows down the sermon. We have to explain why the sower let seed fall on the beaten path. We have to explain wedding customs to make the parable of the wise and foolish virgins make sense. We must talk about the laws governing found treasure, etc. The people in Jesus' day didn't require any explanation.

Perhaps two simple truths will suffice for this section. The first is that the parables are a part of the Gospel. They are not nice little moralistic stories that simply tell us to be kind to others and to be good stewards of our time and talents. The parable of the sower tells us that God's Kingdom will have a harvest. It was a reassuring story for some discouraged disciples. The various marriage feasts and parties described are foreshadowings of the Messianic banquet. To make the story of the laborers in the vineyard a parable about fair wages for all is cheapening Scripture. We do not depart from the Gospel when we present the parables.

The second truth worth noting is that the parables must be adapted at times to the congregation. Jesus was talking to people about coming into the Kingdom. Often we are preaching to people who are already in the Kingdom. Thus a sermon about the prodigal son may involve fervent appeals to the congregation to turn from their sin and turn to God who stands as the waiting father, ready to forgive. But most of the hearers will probably be people who are already in the Kingdom. The figure of the elder brother, sitting in judgment over the returning sinner comes closer to describing most congregational members. So we must look not only at the story but at the audience if we are to make the parables live.

Despite all this, the parables form marvelous preaching material. They should make us reflect that Jesus clothed His messages in pictures, symbols, metaphors. He didn't argue with the man who wanted to know who his neighbor was. He moved around the man's prejudices with a story. The wise preacher should take note here.

The Miracle Stories

There was a time when the miracle stories of the Bible formed easy preaching material. That time is gone. Modern science has raised sceptical questions about all the miraculous stories in the Bible, and timid preachers have backed away from confrontation by adopting all kinds of "natural" explanations for the events described in the Bible. The result is that the preacher is caught in a vise today. There are members who accept the miracles without raising any questions. Indeed some may become miracle mongers like the old lady who heard the minister explain that when Jesus told the man to take up his bed and walk, the bed was simply a bed roll. "No," she insisted, "it was a four-poster, and that was the second miracle in the story." Some people are still like that today.

But there are many in our congregations who raise their eyebrows when the text involves a miracle story. They simply aren't willing to believe that a man who was born blind was given eyesight by Jesus or that water became wine or any of the other miraculous stories in the gospels, much less the stories related in the Old Testament. What is the minister to do?

There is of course a simple solution. Don't preach about miracles. You can avoid them all and still have plenty of texts to preach from. And certainly faith doesn't consist in how many miracles you can believe but in putting your trust in Jesus Christ. The preacher is not like a coach of athletics who puts up a bar and says, "Can you jump over that," and then keeps raising the bar to see how high the person can go.

And yet there is no way that you can eliminate the miraculous from the Bible. From the very beginning, the Scriptures insist that God is involved in this world. He is no absentee landlord. And God's involvement makes the miraculous possible. More than that, Christian truth centers in the death and resurrection of Jesus Christ. Paul's great resurrection chapter in 1 Corinthians makes plain that our faith rises and falls at this point. You may avoid the miraculous for 51 Sundays, but on the 52nd you are caught. And if Christ is risen, then all the other miracles become possible.

Beside this, the miracle stories form part of the heart of the Gospel. You cannot dimiss them and have much Bible left. Thomas Jefferson tried to do that, and the result was grotesque. We would lose some of the most comforting and striking passages of Scripture if we avoided the miracles. Think of the marvelous sequel to Jesus' healing of the man born blind. It is simply fascinating how this unlearned fellow dealt with the Jewish leaders. Or think of the story of the Roman centurion or of the demoniac whose neighbors preferred pigs to human beings. The preacher is foolish if he avoids the miraculous.

But how do we get the message across? First we must see what not to do. The miracles are not to be used to prove anything. They will not convince anyone to accept Jesus as Lord and Savior. Even those who witnessed the miracles did not all believe, and if that didn't do it, we have no chance to win people through miracle stories today. We believe the stories because we believe in Christ, not the other way around. The use of the miraculous to prove Christianity came into vogue in the 18th century, and it was a failure in the age of reason. What chance does such a method have in the age of science? Of course, an apologetic sermon about the resurrection might be of value at times. Paul reminds us that this thing was not done in a corner. But the preacher does not use the miracle to convince those who lack faith. The way of salvation is still Law-Gospel, not miracle-Gospel.

Actually the miraculous material can be used in five different ways. Let's take a look at them. 1. The term "sign" fits better than miracle for the Gospel stories. For every sign points to the same truth—a new age has dawned. The Messiah has come. Note how often the spectators at Jesus' healing marveled and felt that a new prophet had arisen. So each story in a sense says the same thing—look at Jesus. He is the one whom God has sent to redeem mankind.

2. Part of Jesus' work was to show human beings what God was like. He insisted that if men had seen Him, they had seen the Father. The writer of Hebrews picks this up and insists that Jesus "reflects the glory of God and bears the very stamp of His nature." So when we read the story of what Jesus did, we see God in action. Does God care for the poor of this world? Jesus healed the blind beggars, the lepers, the weak, and the impotent. Is God in charge of His world? Jesus stilled the tempest and multiplied the loaves and fishes. One could go on and on. The miracles describe for us very clearly the nature of God. The preacher can make this point about every miraculous story in the gospels.

3. The miracles represent a taste of the future, the *eschaton*. Human beings have always longed for a world in which people would not be born blind, in which leprosy and other diseases would be abolished. They have dreamed of a world in which the poor could be fed and in which even death would be overcome. Jesus through His acts of healing gave men a foretaste of that world. It was a little bit like Camelot, which existed for a while and then fell apart, but in Jesus' case the vision was promised for the future. Lazarus would have to die again, but someday death would be gone. The people healed probably got sick from some other ailment, but not forever. The preacher must not pass by the eschatological element in the miracles.

4. There is also a symbolism behind the miracle stories. This has sometimes been denied because some preachers would reduce all miracles to the symbolic. But there are too many parallels for this symbolism to be denied. Thus sin and leprosy are often identified in the Bible. And the Jesus who could cleanse the lepers could and can cleanse us from sin. Jesus opened the eyes of the blind. But we are blind too and need our eyes opened by His power. Jesus opened the ears of the deaf. But we are deaf too, and He often calls on those who can hear to hear His Word. Note that the church at Laodicea is spoke of as "wretched, pitiable, poor, *blind,* and naked," and that the Lord promises them some salve to anoint their eyes. The symbolic meaning is interwoven with the miracles.

As a matter of fact, these acts of spiritual healing are far greater miracles than the physical ones mentioned in the Bible. That Saul of Tarsus should become the great missionary is more astounding than the healing of ten blind men. The symbolic meaning doesn't lower the miraculous or make it seem commonplace. It does just the opposite, and the preacher should not hold back from this symbolic stress.

5. Every miracle story also carries with it some sidelights that are also valuable for preaching. Think of the faith demonstrated by the woman who was willing to be called a dog but who persisted in seeking help from Jesus. Think of that man by the pool who was so sunken in despair that Jesus had to say to him, "Do you want to be healed?" Think of the terrified disciples in the boat and the rebuke Jesus gave them. No one needs to worry about there being no preaching points in a miracle story. The cast of characters is marvelous although first we

must see the main character, Jesus Himself. The miracles can speak to the church today if the preacher approaches them with the assurance that there is a message for the church in the record of God's action in human history.

The Epistles

The epistles contain excellent preaching material. Although most of them were written before the gospels, they reflect a period after the founding of the church. Thus the message is often closer to the situation of the church today. The epistle texts present a wide range of material from the heavily doctrinal statements to the very practical information about how to live as a Christian in the pagan world. But there are some problems which the preacher must face as he uses an epistle text.

There is little color in the epistles. The gospels are full of interesting stories and fascinating characters. The events are all centered in the land where the Jews lived for centuries. So the congregation may have some familiarity with the setting because they have heard it described before. But the epistles were written to strange places like Corinth and Thessalonica, and no one knows too much about such places. So the preacher has difficulty here in making the text come alive. This is probably the reason so many ministers stay with the gospel pericopes year after year.

In addition we have only one side of a correspondence still available. Many of Paul's writings are in answer to questions that the congregations posed for him through writings or private messengers. But we aren't sure just what the situation actually was. Think of Paul's description of some of the members at Philippi whose "end is destruction, their god is the belly, and they glory in their shame "(Phil. 3:19). Paul knew whom he meant by this description, and undoubtedly the Philippians did, but we are in the dark. Or what was going on there between Euodia and Syntyche, who had to be entreated to agree in the Lord? We simply don't know. The epistles are filled with baffling mysteries.

The epistles are also hard to outline. Nothing is more helpful in preaching than a good, tight outline so that both preacher and congregation can follow what is being said. But epistles are letters, and letters aren't always well organized. Paul particularly has a way of starting with us and then soaring into a great doctrinal statement that is beautiful but perplexing for the preacher. Take a look at Ephesians 4:1-7. The section begins with an appeal to the readers to lead a life "worthy of the calling to which you have been called." But then Paul talks about unity, and this sets him off in a wonderful passage about unity that ends with "one God and Father of us all, who is above all and through all and in all." Just to make it hard, the seventh verse drops back to the idea of diversity of gifts. It is a beautiful text, but the preacher may have trouble knowing where to grab hold.

Although the epistles are written from the background of an organized church, it is also true that they often seem more out of date than the gospels. The problems of first-century Christianity are not necessarily the problems of the church today. We no longer have to worry about eating meat offered to idols, we have no quarrels between Jew and Gentile believers, we do not have to face the problem of slavery or abuses that arose in connection with the love feast. This does not mean that the epistles contain dead texts, but the preacher does have to do more translating of conditions to modern parallels.

Despite all this, the epistles contain fine preaching material. The preacher simply needs to recognize the problems when he uses a pericope from the epistles. One of the real pluses in this kind of preaching is the fine doctrinal material in the writings of Paul and others. The church today is perishing for lack of careful doctrinal preaching. People feel that they want to be on the Lord's side, but they aren't really sure why. Romans, Ephesians, and many other letters will supply that explanation.

However, we need to understand how to do doctrinal preaching. The presentation of abstract dogmatic material will bore a congregation to tears. Many sermons on doctrine belong in the lecture room, not the pulpit. The doctrinal preacher must be sure that his message touches the life of the hearers. Consider, for example, a sermon on the Trinity. Most people are not really concerned whether there are three persons in the Godhead or not. But show them how God has created and still preserves us, indicate how God in Christ saved us, and describe how God's Spirit lives within us and the sermon takes on a different meaning. The doctrinal sections of the epistles are closely tied to the practical advice given by the writers. The preacher should note this fact and make sure that the same close connection is to be found in the Sunday morning sermon.

Sermons from the Old Testament

Recently a layman wrote to ask why preachers didn't preach more often from the Old Testament. He estimated that about 90 percent of the sermons he had heard were from New Testament texts, and the majority of them used the Gospel lesson for their basis. While there is no way to check the statistics, the man's experience is probably an accurate reflection of Lutheran preaching. And the question "Why is this so?" is a legitimate one.

Some answers are obvious. The Old Testament reflects a world that is still further removed from us than are the gospels and epistles. Most of the material reflects the troubles of the Hebrews, their rise and fall, their captivity and return to Palestine, and their waiting for the redeeming of God's promises to deliver them. To a 20th-century audience this all seems very remote and unimportant. It is useful for background but has no meaning for people in the atomic age.

Moreover, when the preacher uses an Old Testament text, he must always admit that there is later news on the subject. You cannot preach from the Old Testament and act as though Christ had not come. For the Christian there is an incompleteness about this earlier material that makes it seem useless today. The nostalgic kick may be all right for antique lovers, but Christians should be